Ready In 10

Written By

Janet Greenwald
&
Laura Greenwald

LION AND THE ROCK
ENTERTAINMENT

For information about special discounts and bulk purchases go to www.getyourstufftogether.com or email us at corpsales@getyourstufftogether.com

Manufactured in the United States of America

ISBN: 978-1536814538

Ready In 10 — Table of Contents

Introduction	Before You Begin	pg. 1
Step 1	Gather Your Documents & Information	pg. 4
Step 2	Record Your Family's Vital Information	pg. 6
Step 3	Record Your Family's Medical Information	pg. 7
Step 4	Store Your Information and Plans	pg. 10
Step 5	Create Your Family's Ready In 10 Plan	pg. 11
Step 6	Turn Your Cell Phone Into A Mobile Command Center	pg. 13
Step 7	Make Emergency Wallet Cards	pg. 16
Step 8	Create Your Family's Evacuation Checklist	pg. 17
Step 9	Create A Get Back To Life Plan	pg. 19
Step 10	Do a Home Inventory/Video Tour	pg. 20
Put It Together	The Finishing Touches	pg. 21
Disaster Mgmt	How To Earthquake Proof Your Bedroom	pg. 22
Three Levels	The Three Levels of Emergencies	pg. 26

This book was inspired by a video that's only five minutes long.

But don't let the short duration fool you. The lessons in it can mean the difference between having what you need and doing without. Being able to thrive, or just barely being able to survive. And, in many cases, it can mean the difference between life and death. It's called the 10 Minute Evacuation Video. Here's how it goes…

We follow a fire truck with lights and sirens blaring, coming down the street. It stops in front of two houses, both middle class families with two or three children. Each time, the firefighter knocks on the front door and tells the families that there's an emergency and they have 10 minutes to evacuate.

Both of the families look startled in the interruption of their day, but that's where the similarities end. One family is ready and one family isn't. A few minutes into the drill, it isn't hard to tell which is which!

The prepared family grabs the plan that they created just in case this ever happened. It has a checklist of things that they need to take with, and the mom and dad quickly divide up the duties – he goes to the home office, she goes to the bedrooms and bathrooms.

Over at the unprepared family's home, chaos is already breaking out. The wife is staring into the bathroom drawers trying to figure out what they need for an undetermined amount of time and the husband is trying to find his shoes and the book he just started reading.

Five minutes into the drill, back at the prepared family home, the photos and vital documents,

pre-packed into a large waterproof plastic bin, have found their way into the car along with the family's computer.

The wife is neatly fitting all of the toiletries, medications, underwear and clothing into two large suitcases, strategically placed on a low shelf of the closet. The kids are sent to pick out two favorite toys and specific items of clothing. As they progress each item is checked off the list.

It's the polar opposite for the unprepared family. Everything's beginning to fall apart. The kids are trying to shove a guitar into the car, dad has now lost his keys and mom is trying to remember where she put the family photos.

Time's up and the prepared family is sitting peacefully in their car, two minutes ahead of schedule. Unprepared family is imagining what would have happened if this had been an actual emergency – like an approaching wildfire. By this time everything vital to their survival, everything important to them, would have been a mass of charred wreckage. Family A, the Prepared Family, took the time to create a plan, to make a checklist and to practice evacuating. Family B? Well they meant to do those things but didn't. Which brings us to the moral of the story…

When something happens, be it your child or husband falling off the garage roof and breaking his leg, a house fire or a full scale natural disaster, life doesn't stop to give you a chance to catch up with the sudden change. It's not like your DVR where you can stop the characters of your favorite drama mid-sentence so you can run and answer the phone.

Life won't give you a few minutes to regroup and catch your breath. If anything, the emergency is just going to get more and more intense until you deal with it. But if you complete each step in this book, you won't need it. You and your family can be ready to evacuate, no matter what the scenario, in 10 minutes or less. And in the next few pages, we'll show you exactly how to do it, quickly and easily.

Before You Begin...

Our mission is for every home to be ready to deal with any disaster or emergency in ten minutes or less. But being "Ready" means different things to different people.

Are You A Type 1 Person?
You live in an area prone to certain disasters, like hurricanes, earthquakes or tornadoes, or you simply want you and your family to be prepared. Your goal is to have your Ready Plans completed, in their notebook and ready to grab and go.

Or Are You A Type 2 Person?
You're facing an imminent emergency. They've just issued a hurricane warning for your area, or the river near your home is reaching flood stage. You just found Ready and need a plan ASAP!

The Ready iin 10 System works no matter what situation you're in.

If you're a **Type 1** person, begin with the Quick Start Guide, and work through each step. The steps themselves should take about 10 minutes each to complete. Then when you have time, go back and fine tune your plans, to make sure that you and your family will have everything you need for future emergencies.

If you're a **Type 2** person, go through the Quick Start Guide to get a general idea of what each plan or checklist does, gather all of your vital documents and information, open and complete or print and fill in the Grab It An Go Vital Documents form, Medical Information Form, Ready Evacuation Plan and the Get Back To Life Plan. Then when the crisis passes, go back, read the book and fine tune your plans, to make sure you have everything you need for future emergencies.

The <u>Right</u> Way To Plan

Imagine that you get a phone call that you've won a free trip to Hawaii. The catch is, you have to be packed, ready and standing at the gate at the airport in 45 minutes. Whether you're a planner by nature or not, you would hang up that phone, grab the nearest suitcase and tear through your house tossing everything you can think of into it, and throw it into the back seat of the car so you can grab that flight.

You get to your hotel, ready to run down to the sparkling, pristine beach only to discover that you have no swim suit, only flip flops, a hat and a half used tube of toothpaste!

That's how most people plan for disasters. They put it off and put it off, until a hurricane warning, a wildfire or a medical emergency rears its ugly head. Then they run through the house throwing things into a suitcase, car or duffel bag and end up with none of the tools or information they really need. Unlike our Hawaii example, not having what you need in an emergency, can literally be the difference between life and death.

How do you keep yourself from ending up the same way? By taking some time right NOW to decide three simple things. If a disaster serious enough to make you evacuate your home, were to strike right now :

- **Where would you go?**
- **Who is going with you?**
- **What do you need to take or have access to?**

In this book, we'll not only take you through **10 steps** that will turn the information **you already have at home** into a detailed disaster action plan, you'll also reap the benefits of the lessons learned through many natural disasters, and learn why being prepared is so absolutely vital, to you and your family.

Ready? Then let's get started.

What's Included With The Ready Book?

Before you begin Step 1, go to:

http://getyourstufftogether.com/download/R10Download.zip

and download the free Grab It And Go Forms and Action Plans that come with this book.

They'll help you document your plans and information so that you can keep them at your fingertips 24/7. They include:

- Financial & Insurance Information Forms
- Medical Information Forms for you and your children
- Emergency Wallet Cards/ID
- Family Evacuation Plan
- Evacuation Checklist
- Your Get Back To Life Plan
- Your Home Inventory

At the beginning of each step, you'll see which document or what supplies are necessary to complete it.

How Do I Use These Forms?

The easiest way to use them is to right click the link to download them to your desktop and fill them out right on your computer.

This way you can save them and edit them later, when changes to your information occur. You can also save them to a portable hard drive, flash drive or password protected online file storage site or family web site, for safekeeping. That way, in the event of an evacuation or emergency, you can take all of your information with you, or you can retrieve it via internet, while you're away from your home computer.

Just remember to save each form with a different name before you begin to fill them out. That way, you'll always have a copy of the originals in case you want to start over.

And one more thing. Even though you only received two adult and two child Grab It And Go Forms, you can easily use them for more than two adults or children, by saving the forms with different names for each member of the family.

You'll also find copies of the forms in the back of this book.

Step 1: Gather Your Documents & Information

As victims of disasters like hurricanes. earthquakes and wildfires have found, being without your birth certificate, bank account numbers or property deeds when you need them most, is a huge problem.   So our first goal is to make your vital information and documents accessible to you while you're away from your home.

Who is going to be evacuating with you? Your spouse, your children? What about parents or relatives?

Your first assignment is to gather all of the vital documents and information that you have for yourself and the loved ones who will be evacuating with you, and sort them into two piles.

What type of info and documents do you need to gather? Here is a list of questions, to get you started:

What types of ID do you and your family members need? Besides driver's licenses and State ID, do you or they have company/school IDs, Medicare/Medicaid cards or health insurance cards?

Do you receive any employee benefits or retirement benefits you might need to access?

Do you have copies of everyone's birth certificates, marriage or divorce certificates?

If you have children, do you have their school records, immunization records, or any other records or IDs that they might need to receive medical, monetary benefits or to re-enroll them in a different school if necessary.

Do you have the contact information for their current school, teachers or school district, to confirm enrollment or past academic history?

What financial information would you need? Do you have the account numbers of all of your bank accounts, customer service numbers, debit card and credit card numbers and service numbers? What about contact information for your lawyer, accountant, broker etc?

Do you have the key to any safe deposit boxes and the information for the box? What about your investment accounts? Do you have investment advisors or financial counselors? Do you have recent credit scores or credit reports you'll need to use for reference?

Do you have all of your insurance and loan information? What about your car, home and any other insurance? Do you have the member numbers, customer service numbers and payment information or web addresses for online billing?

Do you have car or boat or any other kinds of loans? You'll need the numbers and contact information for those as well.

What about the ownership papers or proof of insurance for your vehicles or anything else that you own?

What about your home? If you rent, do you have the all of the contact information for your landlord, including the address of where you send your rent?

If you own property, do you have a copy of your deed, mortgage, the contact information for your mortgage company, representative and payment information?

If you are a landlord, do you have the contact information for all of your tenants and their payment information?

Is there any other information or any other documents we didn't mention, that you would need for your family?

Separate the information you gathered into two piles.

In the **first pile**, place documents that you will actually <u>need to have with you or have access to</u>.

In the **second pile**, place the documents that contain <u>information that you need</u>. For example, you would need to have a copy of the deed to your home, but you wouldn't need a stock certificate – just the account number and contact information for your broker.

In an upcoming step, we will be putting the documents and copies in at least **three** safe, waterproof locations that will be accessible to you during your evacuation.

For now, let's go on to Step 2.

Step 2: Record Your Family's Vital Information

You've already gathered your information. Now it's time to put it work for you.

Supplies: The Financial & Insurance Information Form.

Once you've download the form, go ahead and open it.

You can either type the information directly into the form on the computer, or print it out and fill it in by hand. If you're going to type the information directly into the form, save it with a new name first, so you'll always have the original.

Take all of the information that you gathered in Pile #2, along with your address books and any personal contact lists you have, and fill in as much of the form as possible.

You probably won't need all of the fields – not everyone has three credit cards and two brokerage accounts – but fill in as much information as you can for each section.

If you don't type or don't have a computer, consider having a friend or a relative type, print and save the information for you.

Once you're finished, either save the form to your computer, or if you're filling it in by hand, put it to the side.

Let's go on to Step 3.

What are the most important things you need to survive an emergency evacuation?

● **Enough cash or access to cash to get you through the next several days**

● **Be able to prove your identify to get assistance, or money.**

● **Prove that you own your home, car and other property.**

● **Secure the things that are important to you, including vital documents, important photos/videos, home inventory of your possessions for insurance purposes.**

● **Birth, Death, Marriage certificates**

● **Easy access to your bank accounts, safe deposit accounts, direct deposits and investments**

Step 3: Record Your Family's Medical Information

When a patient is brought in the emergency room unconscious, aside from obvious injuries, the doctors caring for him basically have no information about their patient. They have no idea what he might be allergic to, what medications he's taking or the surgery he had the month before.

When it comes to you and your family, it's up to **you** to fill in that missing piece BEFORE emergencies occur.

Elaine Sullivan was an active seventy-one year old, living on her own in Chicago. One day while getting ready to take a bath, she slipped and fell, striking her head and mouth on the side of the tub. Her neighbors realized they hadn't seen her all day and called the paramedics, who went in and found her, conscious, but unable to speak.

Elaine had been a past patient at the hospital she was taken to, she had private insurance, Medicare and everything she needed. Or so she thought. Even though she was stable, injuries to her mouth made her unable to speak or swallow, so she was unable to speak for herself. Over the next few days, after a series of serious medical errors and a critical drug interaction, her condition worsened.

Elaine Sullivan was my grandma.

Despite the fact that the hospital had my mother's and my contact information for our home in Los Angeles, the hospital neglected to call us for 6 1/2 days. By the time they did, Grandma was in critical condition, from a lack of the most basic care. By the time we found out she'd been hospitalized, we were unable to get to her bedside before she died, unnecessarily and alone.

As we found out the hard way, some hospitals don't make calling your next of kin, their priority.

Even though most hospitals try to find an unconscious patient's emergency contacts and notify their families in a reasonable amount of time, hospital can sometimes become so busy and understaffed, that they don't make that call as quickly as they should.

We later found that one of the main factors that caused Grandma's death was the fact that the doctors treating her didn't have her medical or prescription drug history at their fingertips. All it would have taken was one phone call to us, and they would have had that information.

But the lesson we want to point out is, how critical communicating a person's vital medical information, can be. In the years since, we've found that our story is only the tip of a very deep iceberg. There are hundreds of stories of people who were literally minutes away from the hospital where their family member lay dying, but were never contacted. When the call came it was hours, days or in some cases weeks later, if it came at all. In many cases, just like ours, the loved one died completely and unnecessarily alone.

Recent natural disasters and COVID, have only amplified the need to get a patient's or trauma victim's identification, medical history and emergency contact information as quickly as humanly possible.

Your Emergency Medical Information

There's nothing worse than having something on the tip of your tongue and not being able to remember it – **except** when the word you're trying to remember is the name of a medication, and when the emergency room physician you're speaking to, needs that information to save your daughter's life.

Emergencies can rattle the best of us, and the phone number or facts you know by heart are the very ones that will elude you when you need them most!

Supplies: Your Medical Information Form. There is also a Medical Information Form For Children.

Start by gathering your address book, your insurance information and any medical records or documentation you have hanging around the house. We've included children's forms as well. For older teens, you can use a Child or an Adult form -- whatever fits their needs best.

Before you fill in the form, close your eyes and imagine that you're sitting in the emergency room, with each person, who is evacuating with you. One by one, imagine that your spouse, each child, your parent has an injury, like a broken arm. The doctor – someone you've never seen before and who doesn't know your spouse or child's unique medical or emotional needs – walks through the door. What would you tell the doctor about them? What do you need the doctor to know?

Jot down all of the things that just went through your mind. Old injuries, allergies, surgeries, anything you think is important.

Now picture the same situation, only this time, your loved one is seriously injured and is about to be wheeled into a surgery, he or she might not survive. What does the doctor need to know, to help save your loved one's life?

Keeping all those notes in mind, begin filling out the medical history section, of your Grab It And Go Forms for yourself, your spouse, children and any other adults evacuating with you. If you're typing the forms on the computer, don't forget to rename the forms before you save them.

Once the medical and vital information is complete, choose and name at least three emergency contacts for each person including:

▪ If you are married, include your spouse on your form and yourself on your spouse's form. For all of your emergency contacts, be thorough. Enter all of your home and cell numbers, your email address, IM address and where you can be found on specific days.

▪ Your next contact should be a nearby relative or good friend. Someone who will drop everything to be there with you. This should be someone who you would trust enough to make informed choices on your behalf, if necessary.

▪ Your final contact should be an out of town/out of state relative or friend. In case of regional emergency, even though you can't call within your local calling district, you can often call long distance. A distant friend can be a touch point for the entire family until communication is restored.

Choosing Your Children's Emergency Contacts

In the days after September 11th, two thousand, one hundred children were left stranded in daycare. Why? Because their parents left one question on their emergency contact card empty. What was the question?

"Who should we contact if you are not able to pick up your child?"

How could something so basic, strand two thousand children on one of the scariest days in American history?

Fear.

It was simply the inability (or refusal) to think through what might happen if both parents were unable to reach their child. It doesn't even have to be a life threatening emergency for this to happen. You could be stuck on the freeway, or trapped in an airplane that you were certain would arrive on time.

So take a few moments to think about it. And don't just jot down the first name that pops into your head! If you and your spouse were unable to get to your child for two or three days, who would be the best person to care for him? You need someone who knows your child extremely well. Someone who would be able to calm her down and would have the energy to care for her. Someone who knows what she likes and dislikes. In case of extreme emergency like September 11th, you might need someone with the ability, brains and fortitude to help locate you or your spouse, if overburdened emergency personnel weren't able to help.   That is the kind of thought you need to put into emergency planning, especially where your children are concerned.

When you're finished, you should have one medical form for each adult and child evacuating with you. Save them on your computer, or set them to the side.

Let's go on to Step 4.

Step 4: Store Your Information and Plans

In Step 1 you gathered all of your vital documents and put the ones that you will actually need, in a separate pile. If there is anything else you thought of that needs to be in this pile like a safe deposit key, go get that as well.

Supplies: For this exercise you'll need a large plastic storage bin (as watertight as possible), a scanner or access to a printer/copier and a 1' or 2" ring bound notebook with tabs.

Your goal for this step, is to make these documents, your Action Sheets and Plans, completely accessible to you during an evacuation or an emergency. We're going to store these documents, or copies of them in at least **three** secure, damage-proof locations.

First, scan or make copies of each document.

Scanning is preferable, because you can save a scanned document on your computer, on a portable hard drive or online, making it even more accessible. But if you don't have access to a scanner, make at least two copies of each original document.

▪ The **originals** go in a safe deposit box or water/fireproof safe in your own city.

▪ Place one set of copies in your watertight Plastic Evacuation Bin. Only place the documents that you actually need, in this bin. You'll have access to copies of your vital documents in your safe deposit box, so don't take anything with you, that you would worry about, if it were lost.

▪ Place a second set of copies in a safe deposit box or water/fireproof safe in the city where you'll be evacuating, or with relatives in that location.

If you're concerned about having copies of your vital information out of your sight, scan them instead and place the scans along with your Ready In 10 Document files on a password-protected flash drive or portable hard drive, and store that in the box instead.

▪ We also suggest placing one set of scanned documents and your completed Ready In 10 documents, on a password-protected online file repository or even the file directory of your family's personal web site. This way if you need a copy of your information or forms quickly, you can retrieve them from any Internet-enabled computer.

Second, we're going to create a Ready In 10 Notebook.

As you complete your Forms and Plans, print out a copy, and place it in the ring bound notebook. Each form needs its own tab, so that you can easily find, or replace outdated pages. Any three-ring binder will do in a pinch, but we suggest using one that has a hard, washable, vinyl cover and pockets to catch papers, maps or any other items that can easily become lost.

You now have a Ready In 10 Notebook!

Once you've finished all of the steps and your information is complete, toss the notebook into your Plastic Evacuation Bin for safekeeping.

One important note: DO NOT put your or your family's social security numbers in your list of vital information, or in online files or folders, no matter how secure they are. If you have to have those numbers with you (and haven't memorized them), copy the originals and place the copies in a secure safe deposit box instead.

Let's go on to Step 5.

Step 5: Create Your Family's Evacuation Plan

We have a question for you.

Where will <u>you</u> go when you evacuate?

As you think about the locations you'll use for your evacuation, consider :

- The people travelling with you
- How you'll get there (car, bus, plane)
- Any pets travelling with you
- Whether those locations will actually work for you – for instance are they close to stores or services your family might need, like pharmacies, clothing, banks and doctors

Supplies: Your Family Evacuation Plan.

We suggest that people have three different locations in mind, to give you different types of locations and choices depending on the circumstances.

The top two sections are used to record the people who will be travelling with you, and any special instructions you'll need to gather, in case a disaster or emergency occurs while you're all away from home.

In the next section, write the location that you and your family will use to meet and the location you will use as an evacuation location, if you cannot live in your home, but your immediate area is still safe. Include the address of the location, contact phone, email address and directions.

Next detail the location, address and contact information for the meeting and evacuation locations that your family will use if you not only need to evacuate your home, but your immediate area or city. This might happen during a hurricane or a tornado.

Last, detail the location that your family will use if you need to not only evacuate your city, but your state.

You will also include these locations on your family's emergency wallet cards. Now, no matter what the disaster, even a fire or local emergency, you and your family will now know where and how to gather, and who will be responsible for what, so you can quickly reunite and travel on to your emergency location together. If you like, you can also give a card to the person you chose to be your out-of-area contact as well.

Will you have any pets travelling with you? Be sure to fill out the pet section, so that you will have all the information you need for them, like the name and numbers for the veterinarian, their licenses, and names/numbers of kennels in the location you are evacuating to and any prescriptions or special instructions you'll need until you return home.

> The Family Evacuation Plan
> has two objectives:
>
> To figure out the best location for
> your evacuation
>
> To get you there safely

Finished? Great!

Are you happy with the plans you made? If so, talk them over with your spouse and other people evacuating with you, to get their feedback.

Once the locations and plans are set, you will also be detailing the locations and basic information on your family's emergency wallet card and your family's wallet cards.

If you wish to, you can also give a card to the person you chose to be your out-of-area contact as well.

Saving Your Family Evacuation Plan

Besides placing a copy of your Family Evacuation Plan in your Notebook, put a copy in your files at work and in your computer, or smartphone so you have it with you whenever you might need it. If you have small children, you might want to store a copy of the plan in their school record along with their emergency contact form, or with your children's caregivers. Every six months put a reminder in your calendar to take your family out to breakfast and update all of your emergency plans.

Safe Deposit Boxes

What would we all do without safe deposit boxes, right? They're secure, they provide a place to keep vital information away from home and they're, well, small. Too small sometimes for the things we need to put into them. Not to worry. Just make sure that all of the papers that don't fit into your box are scanned and placed on a flash drive instead.

Let's go on to Step 6.

Step 6: Turn Your Cell Phone Into A Mobile Command Center

Right after Hurricane Katrina and the Tsunami and other recent disasters, someone came up with the idea of putting an ICE entry, (short for In Case Of Emergency), on your cell phone, to make your emergency contacts stand out to emergency workers. Now most hospitals look for ICE entries on the cell phones of unconscious patients.

If a disaster struck right now, where you're sitting and the <u>only</u> thing you could grab was your cell phone, would you have everything you need to:
- Reach the people you love?
- Be able to communicate your vital emergency contacts to emergency personnel?
- Be able to communicate your basic medical information if you are injured and unable to speak for yourself?
- Survive using the information in your phone until you reach home, your loved ones or your pre-planned safe location?

With some thought and planning, you can turn your cell/smartphone into an emergency mobile command center. Not only that, we're going to give you, hospitals and emergency personnel the information necessary to save you or your family member's life, right in your ICE contacts.

As a matter of fact, it's not just the contact names but the contacts themselves who can save your life or provide lifesaving information in an emergency. Recently there was a fire in our neighborhood, that began on the 32nd floor of a high rise condo building. It was one am on one of the coldest nights of the year. The electricity, elevators and regular phone service was out. One woman was not only afraid for herself, but concerned for the ninety year old couple she cared for, who sat huddled nearby.

The apartment was quickly filling with smoke. The problem was, the caregiver had no idea where the fire was.

She called her husband who was in a different state. He got on the internet, found live local news coverage and was able to tell her what floor the fire was on and that the fire department was on the scene. She knew she would be safe for the time being, and was able to wait until the firefighters knocked on their door to lead her and the couple to safety. The moral of the story is to have as many connectivity options available to you as possible. You never know which one might save your life.

Supplies: Your family's Medical Information Forms and your Family Evacuation Plan.

If you have a spouse, relatives or children who will be evacuating with you, update their cell phones first. Use the two main emergency contacts from each family member's Medical Information Forms. Depending on the cell phone model, you should be able to put quite a bit of information right in each of those contacts. The contact name of course will be ICE, but you can put the contact's first name and relationship, (for example Cynthia – Mom) in the company name field, so a doctor reading it, would know that this contact is the patient's mother.

Play around with the other fields, until you fill in all the information you possibly can. For example:

- Your emergency contact's main phone number
- Cell number
- Work number
- Email Address
- IM, Twitter and Facebook address in case so you can send each other emergency messages or quick updates
- A direct URL link to a document containing the owner of the phone's full emergency contact information and basic medical history

You'll find ICE instructions in your download files.

If you have a smartphone, you can also save your Family Evacuation Plan as a file on your phone, or simply type the details of your family's evacuation locations into a second or third contact on their phones. This way, if disaster strikes while they're away from home, each member of the family will always have the locations, phone numbers and other vital information at their fingertips.

On your own phone, list your ICE contacts the same way. If you have a smartphone, you can also store copies of your family's medical history forms, checklists and Family Evacuation Plan, right on your phone. Since **you** are your family's Mobile Command Center, make sure you enter the cell numbers, email addresses, text addresses of the people evacuating with you and any other reference numbers you might need while evacuated.

Living In A State of Constant Communication

In the middle of a busy, but quiet day in a Midwestern university lecture hall, the silence was suddenly pierced by a hail of gunfire. Students ran out of the hall and ducked under tables. Those who couldn't move tried to make themselves as invisible as possible until help arrived. That day at Northern Illinois University, five students lost their lives and many others were injured. As the police and security were struggling to control the situation, **a few people were able to find out what was happening, in real time**. They were blessed to know that their children or classmates were all right.

The NIU Shootings – Facebook and Twitter to the Rescue

So how did some parents and friends have a real time view of the NIU tragedy? Facebook and Twitter! As unbelievable as it sounds, students ingeniously found a way to use their favorite method of keeping in touch with friends, as a tool to connect to the outside world in time of crisis.

Students caught under desks and tables grabbed their smart phones and started communicating. Tweets went out on Twitter, notes and messages went up on Facebook pages. Messages told friends and family that the students who were literally in the thick of things, were all right.

Others told loved ones or security officers where trapped students were located, facilitating their rescue. Friends started texting each other to find out where everyone was and in the hours that followed, created Facebook pages memorializing the fallen.

It was an amazing display of people, used to being in touch with friends 24/7, using that same technology to communicate, connect, survive and heal.

Smart phones, cell phones and notebook computers are a GREAT way to stay in touch during an emergency. Whether you send a simple email or text, or send tweets or post to each other's Facebook walls, in seconds you can find out the location of everyone you love, discover if they're all right, or need help, and even mobilize family and friends to be at the side of the ill or injured. In a dire emergency you can even confirm or update emergency plans like meeting places, using real time information.

Most importantly technology can bring your loved ones together, just when you need each other the most. That was just demonstrated in the 7.0 earthquake in Haiti. Here's a quote from CNN: "*Communication with people in Haiti was, at best, sketchy and achieved mainly through social networking sites such as Twitter and YouTube and via Internet phone.*"

So how can your family use technology in an emergency?

When you created your Family Evacuation Plan, you made sure that you gathered each family member's email addresses, text, user names and cell numbers on the plan. You need to take that one step farther by making sure by giving each member of the family that information.

Their "homework" will be to enter one contact on their cell phone for each member of the family, containing all of that information.

You would be surprised how many people have entries for every friend and colleague they've had since camp, only to be missing the most vital information for members of their own family! I guess we just always assume that the people we love most will be standing right next to us, the moment a disaster strikes. But this exercise will ensure that even if they aren't right next to you, that you'll be reunited as quickly as humanly possible.

When your plan is complete, sit down with your family to discuss the ways you can all use technology to stay in touch with each other during a disaster. Come up with some sample scenarios, for example, if a disaster were to happen while your family members were at work, at school or running errands during a normal day.

How would you connect with each other?

Would you text each other, or would calling be faster?

If you have teens or young adults at home, their natural proclivity may be to send out a tweet on Twitter, to update everyone they know on their location or situation.

Don't forget Twitter can also be used to send personal messages, so you don't have to worry about broadcasting your personal business for the entire world to read.

Suppose cell phones were out, but electricity was working, or vice versa. The best way to plan, is to give yourselves as many ways as possible to stay connected. Then if one or two normal methods are unusable, you'll all simply turn to a different method to reach each other.

Another idea is to create a Family Emergency Code or Word. This is a code or word that only you and your immediate family know. When a family member says it, texts it or emails it to the rest of the family, it signals that they're in trouble or need help immediately. It's only to be used in extreme emergency and means that everyone needs to drop what they're doing and establish contact immediately.

In the last few years, the world has changed dramatically. There are tools and resources available to you and your family that you were unimaginable in the last decade. The best thing about it, is that every family now has the opportunity to communicate and stay in touch in the way that's best for them.

Let's go on to Step 7.

Step 7: Make Emergency Wallet Cards

No one will ever be able to forget the pictures of the thousands of people simply wandering after Katrina or the Haiti earthquake, because they became separated from their families or friends during the chaos of the disaster.

One of the best ways to prevent this from happening to your family, is to give each person evacuating with you their own Emergency Wallet Card. Traditionally wallet cards include a person's name, address and phone number, along with a few emergency contacts. But of course, we're about to kick it up a notch!

Supplies: Your Emergency Wallet Cards.

Once you download the emergency wallet cards you can either fill them out right on your computer, or you can print them out and fill them in by hand. It's up to you.

Creating them on the computer, is the best way to do it, if you can. This way the information is easier to read, and the cards can be saved, edited or reprinted, any time you need them.

Go ahead and fill in at least one card for yourself and each person evacuating with you. Notice that the cards not only have space for the card holder's name and emergency contacts, but they also have room for out of area emergency contacts, insurance information, emergency locations from your Evacuation plan, and a link to the card holder's basic medical history.

Once the cards are complete, print them out and put them into a plastic lanyard (around the neck) card holder, or a Shoewallet, and put them into your Plastic Evacuation Bin. Placing the wallet card into a card holder will not only keep it safe and dry, but make it easy to wear and locate during evacuation.

Let's go on to Step 8.

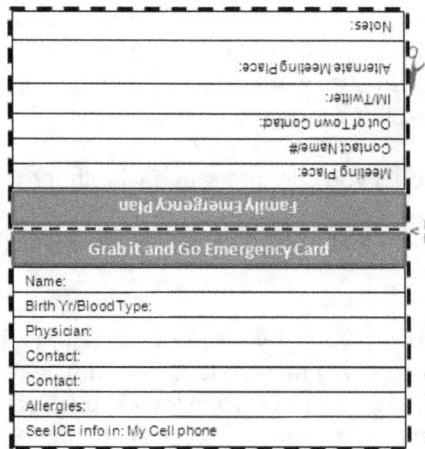

Step 8: Create Your Family's Evacuation Checklist

Now that you know where you're going and how you're going to get there, it's time to put together your Evacuation Checklist.   Your checklist should include everything that you and the people travelling with you can't do without, and can't easily replace, like contact lenses, or extra set of car keys.

Supplies: Your Evacuation Checklist

Go ahead and download, then open the Checklist.

The first section on the list is for things you need to do before you leave the house, like turning off the water or unplugging appliances -- anything you would normally do before or after a disaster.

The next section is the checklist of items that you will be taking with you. On it, there is a place for the name of the item, its location and the person responsible for grabbing it and seeing that it finds its way into the box, suitcase or car. This way everyone will know who is responsible for what, instead of everyone grabbing for the same item and forgetting others.

Below is a list of items to get you started, but please make sure that your list reflects the needs of your family.

You'll also need to bring extra eyeglasses/ contact lenses, prescription medications and the prescriptions that accompany them. This is also a good time to encourage you to fill all of your recurring prescriptions at a nationwide pharmacy chain, like Walgreens, CVS or Rite-Aid. That way if you need to evacuate and realize you've run out of a medication, you can have your prescription replaced without having to go to a local physician.

Next list all the keepsakes you need to take with you. This includes photo albums/family histories, journals, diaries, a few favorite pieces of clothing and cherished books. As you list each one, note where it is located. Can you find this item quickly? If something is important enough to you to take with you in an evacuation, it shouldn't be that hard to find! If you display it where you can see or use it, you'll be able to retrieve it when necessary.

Don't forget to ask the people evacuating with you for their list of 5-10 keepsakes and add them to your checklist. For the next few days, pay attention to the things you and your family regularly use. If you identify other items that you can't do without, add them to the checklist.

Another thing to consider is the place to which you'll be evacuating. Is there anything that the location doesn't have that you'll need when you get there?

First aid supplies	Diapers, infant formula	Ready Notebook
Cash	Toys/things to keep children occupied	Flash drive/portable hard drive containing vital documents
House/Car Keys	Flashlight, Batteries, Tools	Journals, diaries, letters,
Toiletries	Cell phone, Battery operated radio	ID and Wallet Cards for everyone traveling Insurance/Medicare cards
Comfortable weather-appropriate clothing	Tools, gloves	Keepsakes or anything unable to be replaced

Is there anything on your list, that they will have, that you really don't need to take with you? If you'll be evacuating to the home of a relative, consider leaving a box of emergency items with them the next time you visit. That way if you do have to evacuate, you'll have less to remember and carry with you. Will you have access to a computer and the Internet at that location? If not, consider getting a small netbook computer to take with you to keep you in touch with people back home, news updates and access to online bill pay, financial accounts and to vital documents/information in your online files or family websites.

The last section is a short list of Emergency Supplies. There are many terrific resource guides on the things you and your family would need to live through a storm or earthquake, by riding it out in your home. You'll find links to many of them in *Top Tech Toys* in your download folder.

Let's go on to Step 9.

Step 9: Create A Get Back To Life Plan

Scene One: You and your family are in your evacuation location two days after the hurricane subsides. The phone rings. It's a good friend of yours, who has just toured your neighborhood and is calling to tell you that your home is badly damaged and he doubts that you will be able to live in it for several months, if ever again. After you and your family hold each other and talk for a few days, you finally feel strong enough to open your Ready In 10 Notebook. There you find your Get Back To Life Plan and begin making calls to your insurance agent, your contractor and your boss. You call the local real estate agent in your evacuation city and ask her to begin looking for temporary housing, register your children in the local school, and begin calling the contacts you need (that you jotted down just in case), to help you settle in.

Getting settled is easier than you thought, since you have copies of all of the vital documents you need, like your birth certificates and property deeds in a safe deposit box at the local bank. It takes some time, but with hard work and a lot of courage, you and your family are back to living in a matter of weeks.

Scene Two: You and your family are in your evacuation location two days after the hurricane subsides. The phone rings. It's a good friend of yours, who has just toured your neighborhood and is calling to tell you that your home is badly damaged and he doubts that you will be able to live in it for several months, if ever again. After you and your family hold each other and talk for a few days, you realize that you have no idea what you're going to do.

Same scenario, same challenges, **one difference**. One path comes with a **plan** for finding your way back.

Supplies: Your Get Back To Life Plan

Facing a disaster without giving yourself a plan to recover from it, is like trying to build a house with no blueprint and no tools!

Download, then open the Get Back To Life Plan file and print it out. In the first section, you'll find a list of questions to guide you through the decisions you'll have to make as you create your plan.

Take a few moments to think about your answers, and do a draft in pencil. Once your plan is set, go ahead and fill in your answers.

In the second section, is space for your actual plan. Once you're ready, go ahead and fill that in as well.

In the final section, compile a list of real estate agents, financial contacts and jobs, schools, doctors and other professionals or information that you might need to establish yourself in the new city temporarily or permanently.

Your Evacuation Quicklist

Go ahead and download, then open your Evacuation Quicklist. Here, you'll find space to record any contacts that you might need in an emergency, that didn't make the cut on your vital information or medical forms. For example, you can include the names of people you deal with every day, like good friends or your favorite service people. If you're evacuated, you might have to call your plumber or neighbor before you return, to look for damage to your home or take care of emergency repairs.

When your Get Back To Life Plan and Quicklist are complete, print a copy and place it in the back of your Ready In 10 Notebook.

Let's go on to Step 10.

Step 10: Do a Home Inventory/Video Tour

Supplies: Your Home Inventory List

The Home Inventory List, gives you a detailed look at the valued items in your home, along with a short description, the manufacturer, serial number and warranty information.

Print a copy of the list, and fill it out in pencil as you walk around your home.

Once the list is complete, take a few moments to videotape a walking tour of your home, highlighting valuables, furniture or electronics that would be expensive to replace. If they are damaged in a disaster, you'll have proof of the item's original condition to give to the claims adjuster, as well as a way to jog your memory of the things that would need to be replaced. If you aren't able to videotape them, take photos instead.

When the form and walking tour are complete, place a copy of the home inventory in your Ready In 10 Notebook, and copies of the document with the walking tour in your safe deposit box locations, portable hard drive/flash drive or online file repository.

Putting It All Together

And that's it. Place your completed Notebook in your Plastic Evacuation bin, in a safe, easy to retrieve area of your home like your laundry room or garage. In that bin, you can also place items from your Evacuation Checklist like extra socks, an old pair of eyeglasses, an umbrella, pencils and paper, toiletries and a first aid kit. Any items that will give you a head start on packing, but won't go bad.

This is also be a great place to store your extra family photos or your emergency portable hard drive or flash drive. Not only will they already be in the plastic bin for easy evacuation, but you'll be able to find them if you need to look through the photos or update the information on your flash or hard drive.

If you've also saved electronic versions of the forms and plans on your computer, remember to save them in the safe locations you identified back in Step 4.

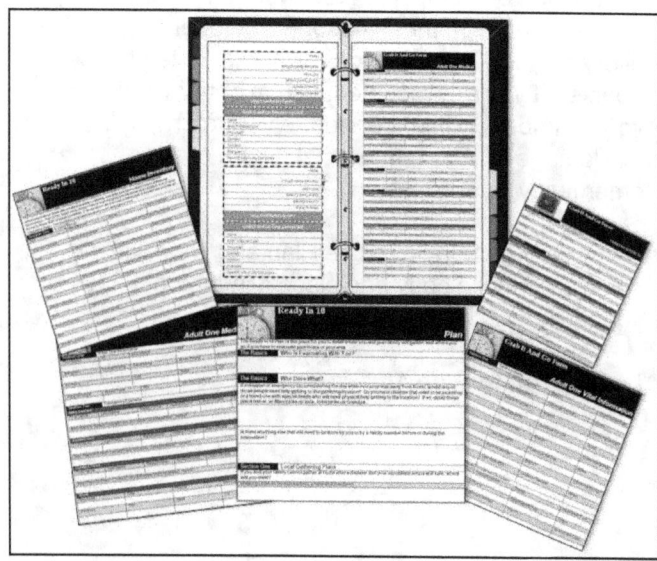

The Finishing Touches

If you live in earthquake or hurricane country, don't forget to keep a set of emergency supplies in your car and a larger supply at work. Many companies already have emergency bins in California and Florida with enough water, first aid supplies and even dried food for two or three days, for each employee.

Now that you've completed the exercises, action plans and Grab It And Go Forms, you're <u>almost</u> there.

What do we mean almost? Well Ready In 10 is a great start, but as you've seen in the pages, you still need a few tools and products to help you prepare for or survive a disaster.

Problem is, how do you know WHICH tools will help you BE completely prepared? Tools like sturdy, reliable portable hard drives and flash drives to secure your data. Flashlights, portable TVs and weather/emergency radios to provide light and up-to- the-minute disaster information. Netbook computers and universal chargers. Disaster kits, notebooks and tabs. Even quick, easy ways to save or back up your treasured photos and music.

We've got you covered. Download our ***Top Tech Toys*** to find a list of the top rated, most recommended products in those categories and more.

This is Only A Drill

This is also the perfect time to mention that completing your plan is a great first step, but practice makes perfect. That may sound a little cliché, but studies show that families who hold a mock fire drill or in our case a mock evacuation drill, are much more likely to do well in a real evacuation. If you have kids, make it into a game, like a treasure hunt, to see how fast each member of the family can gather the items on his or her list and get everything into the car. That way, if the real thing happens, you'll be working from muscle memory. You'll already have the picture of yourselves doing this successfully and it won't be as big a deal as trying your system out for the first time, when you HAVE to get out of the house. Another benefit of rehearsing is that you'll be able to pinpoint things that don't work, and be able to fix them before you are actually facing an evacuation.

Since everyone's information changes so quickly these days, it's also a great idea to set aside an hour once or twice a year to look over your plans any update any out of date or incorrect information. For example a new credit card number, or a relative's new address or phone number. To make it even easier to remember, make the day you do your drill and update your plan the same day that you change the clocks back, or the day after a big family gathering.

How To Earthquake Proof Your Bedroom

Even though Melanie grew up in Southern California, when she actually felt an earthquake for the first time, she didn't know what to do first.

And if you've ever gone through an earthquake you know what she means. Our first "real" shaker was the Whittier quake and it was so strong it had me pinned to the bed. That's why it's so important to have the things you need at your fingertips, before the quake strikes.

One of the reasons that earthquakes are so hard to prepare for is that they tend to happen very early in the morning. Imagine being shaken out of a sound sleep, only to realize that your bed, your walls and your floor are all moving in opposite directions, while you helplessly try to remember the first item on your disaster checklist.

Which is why Melanie was running around pulling thing after thing out of her closet yelling, "WHERE ARE MY EARTHQUAKE CLOTHES???!!!"

Of course, a few minutes later she realized she didn't even need to leave her house the whole wardrobe thing ended up being a non-issue. What she was really looking for was a way to regain a sense of control. Her way of doing that just happened to be fashion.

As longtime residents of Southern California we know how hard people work to get their offices, their homes and their garages ready for an earthquake. But since most earthquakes happen in the wee hours of the morning, people don't have their basic supplies where they need to be. Their bedroom. So let's take care of that right now.

There are two things to keep in mind while making your bedroom earthquake safe.

Safety and Communication.

Safety

Make your bedroom as safe as possible, during and after an earthquake, by storing earthquake and first aid supplies near your bed and anchoring items and furniture that might fall or break.

Your Emergency Kit

First, get a sturdy metal or heavy plastic box to hold your basic emergency supplies. Make sure that it closes well and is heavy enough to stay where you put it, even during intense shaking.

Put it directly under your bed, so that you can grab it easily without having to get out of the bed.

In this box, place:

A whistle, a few protein bars, a few bottles of water, a small flashlight, small emergency radio, a first aid kit and a portable charger that will give you extra battery life for cell phones. The rest of your supplies – whatever you feel would be necessary for you and your family – can go into the closet beneath your earthquake clothes.

Next to the box, place a pair of rubber-soled shoes for you and your spouse. If you have kids, their shoes and a small flashlight should go under their beds.

The instant an earthquake wakes you – especially if it's one that causes a lot of damage – put your shoes on before you get out of bed. There might be broken glass or debris on the floor. That goes double if you have to leave your home. Outside you could encounter rocks, pieces of brick from chimneys or downed power lines.

The Closet

Choose a generic earthquake outfit. If it's cold out, jeans and a sweatshirt or warm sweater, plus a warm jacket and socks.

If it's warmer, jeans, light layers and a light jacket and socks. If you have to leave your home, you won't necessarily get back in for hours or days. Store that outfit together at the end of your closet nearest to your bed, so you can grab the clothes and put them on without wasting time thinking about it. As much as we love you Melanie, this is no time for high fashion!

Right below your earthquake clothes, place a small box with the rest of your earthquake supplies.

This should include a hand-crank or battery powered radio, a larger flashlight, extra batteries, a few more bottles of water, high calorie or high protein food that will stay fresh for a year, a can opener (the one we love opens cans without leaving sharp edges), a small stash of cash, and if you have one, a portable television with an antenna. One other thing you can include is a small generator.

If anyone in your family needs glasses, contact lenses or prescription drugs, throw those in as well. If they or you need refrigerated insulin, consider buying a small portable refrigerator for your bedroom. Even if the electricity goes out, the refrigerator will remain cold enough for a few hours, until you can get help. Then place a reminder on your calendar every few months, to recycle the perishable items in your kit with fresh items.

Furniture

Make sure all of the cabinets, pictures, mirrors, televisions and anything else breakable in your bedroom are anchored down, so they don't turn into earthquake driven torpedoes that can harm you or your family. Carol Burnett had a close call during the Northridge Quake when a television flew off her bookcase and landed on her bed. Even though she always laid on that side, that night she had trouble sleeping and switched to the other side of the bed!

The best things we've found to anchor furniture and breakable objects without harming them is Quakehold.

Quakehold straps secure furniture like bookcases while blending right into your decor.

Do you have breakable figurines, picture frames or glass keepsakes in bookcases or on dressers? If so, anchor the bottom of the keepsake to the surface with Quakehold Museum Wax. It holds items securely to a surface without harming either. And if it's in a bookcase, be sure to affix the keepsake to the back of the bookcase as well for extra safety.

If you have the space, move a heavy piece of furniture into your bedroom that you and your spouse can use for shelter during a quake. A heavy table or a desk you can both fit under is ideal.

Communication

Make sure you can easily connect with the world around you, from your bedroom.

After an earthquake, if the electricity is still on, turn on the TV or radio, so you'll have a friendly voice there in the room with you and you won't feel isolated or alone. Besides true Angelenos always bet on how big the earthquake was and never go back to bed until they hear Dr. Kate Hutton's report on the preliminary magnitude from Cal Tech, so they can see who won.

Keep one cell phone in the room with you at night, where you can easily reach it. And get into the habit of plugging it into the charger when you get home in the evening so it will always be ready to go whenever you need it.

You're probably wondering why we mentioned putting a whistle in your emergency kit. When the Northridge earthquake hit, many apartment residents were trapped in their bedrooms and had to be rescued. A whistle can help you communicate your location to rescue teams. That and a cell phone with GPS are both are a good idea.

If you have a landline phone, keep it. Cell phones are great, but the chances of cell towers being down after an earthquake are much more likely than phone lines being inoperable. And even if they're up and running, cell traffic, tweeting, Instagram and texting skyrocket after an earthquake, overwhelming the circuits.

Give yourself as many alternate ways of communicating as possible. Preferably a mobile phone, smartphone, landline phone and a notebook, iPad, or tablet with Wi-Fi access.

Don't forget, that if you need to check on local friends or relatives, it's usually easier to call long distance numbers, than local numbers after an earthquake. It's smart to appoint an out of town contact for all of your family members to check in with, until your communications within the quake zone return to normal.

Taking a few minutes to make your room earthquake friendly now, can make all the difference when you really need it. And if you're ready to take organizing to the next level, be sure to pick up a copy of our book *Keep The Stuff You Love Safe*.

The Three Levels of Emergencies

When something unexpected happens, whether your spouse falls off the roof, a jumbo jet crashes across the street from your home, or Hurricane Katrina is barreling full force towards your city, you are thrown into crisis mode. But after all, a crisis is a crisis. So whatever the emergency is that you'll face, you'll need to react to it in basically the same way, right?

Wrong!

The only thing those three emergencies have in common is that they can definitely throw you for a loop. But if you look at them closely, you'll realize that the tools you need to respond to them are entirely different. The spouse falling off the roof scenario is a **Level 1 Emergency**. You'll need to grab your spouse's medical history, insurance cards, get someone to watch the kids and call the paramedics.

The airplane crash, is a **Level 2 Emergency**. You'll have to evacuate, which means grabbing what you and your family need to have with you for the next few days physically, financially and emotionally, secure your home, gather the family at a predetermined meeting place and stay away from home until it's safe to return.

A hurricane like Katrina or an earthquake like Haiti, is a **Level 3 Emergency**. Not only will you have to evacuate, you will have to face the possibility of physical danger during evacuation, injuries to yourself or your family, you will also have to secure your home, with no guarantee that you will ever see it or be able to live in it, ever again. You might very well have to start your life over, in a different city and need every shred of vital information that you have, to do that successfully.

On the next page, you'll find a chart that tells you which forms/plans you'll need for which type of emergency.

The inspiration for this book might have come from a ten minute evacuation drill video, but the inspiration for our entire series of safe family and student action plans, came from an experience that touched our own family. It's the perfect example for a Level 2 Disaster.

The day started like any other. I was a stay at home mom, and had just finished a load of laundry, before preparing dinner. As I opened the cabinet to reach for a dish, the house shuttered. It felt like something had hit the roof -- hard. A moment later there was an enormous roar, followed by a shock wave. The kitchen chairs flew across the room and everything was cascading off the countertop. I ran to the living room window and pulled back the curtains. All I could see was orange – everything was orange. I closed the curtains and opened them again, thinking I had to be imagining it. But I wasn't.

As I stared out the window I realized that the orange was actually a ball of fire surrounding what remained of a 737, lying broken, smoke billowing, just across the street and two houses away from where I stood. The houses under the airplane were nothing more than rubble. I immediately searched the distance for my daughter's school just two blocks away. From what I could see beyond the smoke, it looked okay. Adrenaline took over. We'd need clothes – at least one night and one day's worth for Laura, my husband and my mother who lived with us.

We'd need cash – whatever we had in the house, ID. Pictures? At least a few and a credit card…

By this time I was running from room to room dumping everything I needed on the couch. There was a knock at the door. "We're evacuating the neighborhood", said a fireman in full gear. "Take everything you need for the next two or three days."

"You have five minutes."

Our family survived the plane crash that day. Those across the street, did not. We were and continue to be very blessed. But those five minutes to grab whatever I could were some of the most stressful and most difficult I've ever experienced.

Ready In 10 was designed to keep you and your family from experiencing the same thing that we and countless other families have experienced.

Now that you've completed all of the exercises and put your Notebook together, you have everything that you need to Grab and Go the moment you need it. When an emergency or disaster occurs, all you have to do is decide what type of emergency it is, open your Notebook and grab the information you need from the grid below, and go.

You're Done!

Congratulations on a job well done! You are now at least ninety percent more prepared than anyone else in your neighborhood. And sleep well tonight – you deserve it!

For more information on disaster preparedness, or keeping your family or hospital patients safe in an emergency, visit our resource site Connected at rnn10.wordpress.com.

Or to read more about our other books, go to www.getyourstufftogether.com

Adult One - Medical

Section One — **Adult One Information**

First Name	MI	Last Name	M/F	DOB

Religion	Home Phone	Cell Phone	Work Phone	Email Address

Address		City	State	Zip

Height/Weight	Blood Type	RH	Identifying Marks	

Section Two — **Emergency Contacts**

Main Contact:

First Name	Last Name	Relationship	Home Phone	Work Phone	Cell

Best Place to Reach Contact? Any Schedule Considerations? Notes?

Contact Two

First Name	Last Name	Relationship	Home Phone	Work Phone	Cell

Best Place to Reach Contact? Any Schedule Considerations? Notes?

Contact Three

First Name	Last Name	Relationship	Home Phone	Work Phone	Cell

Best Place to Reach Contact? Any Schedule Considerations? Notes?

Work

Employer	Title	Phone	Manager

Address	City	State	Zip

Section Three — **Medical Information**

Primary Physician	Specialty	Phone	Alt Phone/Email	Hospital

Physician Two	Specialty	Phone	Alt Phone/Email	Hospital

Physician Three	Specialty	Phone	Alt Phone/Email	Hospital

Dentist	Specialty	Phone	Alt Phone/Email	Notes

Dentist Two	Specialty	Phone	Alt Phone/Email	Notes

Optometrist	Glasses/Contacts?	Phone	Alt Phone/Email	Location

Section Four	Prescription, Allergy & Chronic Condition Information

Prescription Information

Prescription Name	Dosage	Frequency	For what condition

Prescription Name	Dosage	Frequency	For what condition

Prescription Name	Dosage	Frequency	For what condition

Prescription Name	Dosage	Frequency	For what condition

Name of Pharmacy	Phone	Pharmacist	Location

Allergy Information

Allergy Type	Severity	Frequency/Last Occurrence/Notes

Allergy Type	Severity	Frequency/Last Occurrence/Notes

Allergy Type	Severity	Frequency/Last Occurrence/Notes

Chronic Conditions

Condition	Severity	Current Treatment/Notes

Condition	Severity	Current Treatment/Notes

Condition	Severity	Current Treatment/Notes

Immunizations

Immunization	Date	Immunization	Date

Immunization	Date	Immunization	Date

Immunization	Date	Immunization	Date

Section Five	Health Insurance

Insurance Company	Member Number	Group/Policy Number	Customer Service

Member Hospital	Agent Name	Agent Number	Notes
Insurance Company	Member Number	Group/Policy Number	Customer Service
Member Hospital	Agent Name	Agent Number	Notes

Section Six	Do You Have A….		
Will?	Location	Power of Attorney?	Location
Living Will/Trust?	Location	Other	Location

Section Seven   **Important Things To Know**

Things I want an emergency physician to know about me

Things I want an emergency physician to know about my medical history

Any other notes, important numbers or wishes that need to be communicated

Section Eight   **Recent Medical Procedures and Tests**

Procedure 1	Date	Reason for Procedure
Physician	Hospital	Results
Procedure 2	Date	Reason for Procedure
Physician	Hospital	Results
Medical Test 1	Date	Reason for Procedure
Physician	Hospital	Results
Medical Test 2	Date	Reason for Procedure
Physician	Hospital	Results
Medical Test 3	Date	Reason for Procedure
Physician	Hospital	Results

Section Nine		Alternative Medicines and Other Substances Commonly Used	
Vitamins or Herbs Taken	Dosage	Frequency/Last Occurrence/Notes	
Vitamins or Herbs Taken	Dosage	Frequency/Last Occurrence/Notes	
Vitamins or Herbs Taken	Dosage	Frequency/Last Occurrence/Notes	
Substances or Alcohol Used	Frequency	Substances or Alcohol Used	Frequency
Substances or Alcohol Used	Frequency	Substances or Alcohol Used	Frequency
Substances or Alcohol Used	Frequency	Substances or Alcohol Used	Frequency

Section Ten		Counselors or Other Health Providers	
Counselor 1	Specialty	Phone	Alternate Phone
Counselor 2	Specialty	Phone	Alternate Phone

Section One — Child One Information

First Name	MI	Last Name	M/F	DOB

Religion	Home Phone	Cell Phone	Notes

Address	City	State	Zip

Height/Weight	Blood Type	RH	Identifying Marks

Section Two — Emergency Contacts

Parent/Guardian One:

First Name	Last Name	Relationship	Home Phone	Work Phone	Cell Phone

Best Place to Reach Contact? Any Schedule Considerations? Notes?

Parent/Guardian Two:

First Name	Last Name	Relationship	Home Phone	Work Phone	Cell Phone

Best Place to Reach Contact? Any Schedule Considerations? Notes?

Contact Three

First Name	Last Name	Relationship	Home Phone	Work Phone	Cell Phone

Best Place to Reach Contact? Any Schedule Considerations? Notes?

School

School	Phone	Teacher	Grade

Address	City	Notes

Babysitter	Phone	Afterschool Program #	Phone

Section Three			Medical Information		
Primary Pediatrician		Specialty	Phone	Alt Phone/Email	Hospital
Physician Two		Specialty	Phone	Alt Phone/Email	Hospital

Dentist	Specialty	Phone	Alt Phone/Email	Notes
Optometrist	Glasses/Contacts?	Phone	Alt Phone/Email	Location

Section Four		Prescription, Allergy & Chronic Condition Information	

Prescription Information

Prescription Name	Dosage	Frequency	For what condition
Prescription Name	Dosage	Frequency	For what condition
Prescription Name	Dosage	Frequency	For what condition
Prescription Name	Dosage	Frequency	For what condition
Name of Pharmacy	Phone	Pharmacist	Location

Allergy Information

Allergy Type	Severity	Frequency/Last Occurrence/Notes
Allergy Type	Severity	Frequency/Last Occurrence/Notes
Allergy Type	Severity	Frequency/Last Occurrence/Notes

Chronic Conditions

Condition	Severity	Current Treatment/Notes
Condition	Severity	Current Treatment/Notes

Immunizations

Immunization	Date	Immunization	Date
Immunization	Date	Immunization	Date
Immunization	Date	Immunization	Date

Section Five		Health Insurance	
Insurance Company	Member Number	Group/Policy Number	Customer Service
Member Hospital	Agent Name	Agent Number	Notes
Insurance Company	Member Number	Group/Policy Number	Customer Service
Member Hospital	Agent Name	Agent Number	Notes

Section Six	What I want an Emergency Physician to Know About My Child

What you need to know about my Child's Medical History

What you need to know about my Child's Personality

These are my Child's Likes and Dislikes

What Calms Her or Him Down

These are my child's Food Preferences and Bedtime Routines

Anything else I want you to know about my child

Section Seven	Recent Medical Procedures and Tests	
Procedure 1	Date	Reason for Procedure
Physician	Hospital	Results
Procedure 2	Date	Reason for Procedure
Physician	Hospital	Results
Medical Test 1	Date	Reason for Procedure
Physician	Hospital	Results
Medical Test 2	Date	Reason for Procedure
Physician	Hospital	Results

Section Eight	Alternative Medicines and Other Substances Commonly Used	
Vitamins or Herbs Taken	Dosage	Frequency/Last Occurrence/Notes
Vitamins or Herbs Taken	Dosage	Frequency/Last Occurrence/Notes
Vitamins or Herbs Taken	Dosage	Frequency/Last Occurrence/Notes

Section Nine	Counselors or Other Health Providers		
Counselor 1	Specialty	Phone	Alternate Phone
Counselor 2	Specialty	Phone	Alternate Phone

GET YOUR
STUFF TOGETHER

Financial Information

Bank Accounts

Bank	Account Number	Branch	Checking/Savings
Website	User Name/PIN	Customer Service	Notes
Bank	Account Number	Branch	Checking/Savings
Website	User Name/PIN	Customer Service	Notes
Bank	Account Number	Branch	Checking/Savings
Website	User Name/PIN	Customer Service	Notes
Bank	Account Number	Branch	Checking/Savings
Website	User Name/PIN	Customer Service	Notes

CDs and Investment Accounts

Institution	Account Number	Branch	Investment Type
Broker/Counselor	Phone	Rate/Maturity Date	Notes
Institution	Account Number	Branch	Investment Type
Broker/Counselor	Phone	Rate/Maturity Date	Notes

Section Three — IRA/401K/Retirement Accounts

Institution	Account Number	Branch	Type

Broker/Counselor	Phone	Notes

Institution	Account Number	Branch	Type

Broker/Counselor	Phone	Notes

Institution	Account Number	Branch	Type

Broker/Counselor	Phone	Notes

Section Four — Credit Cards

Company	Account Number	Website	User Name/PIN

Credit Limit	Interest Rate	Customer Service	Notes

Company	Account Number	Website	User Name/PIN

Credit Limit	Interest Rate	Customer Service	Notes

Company	Account Number	Website	User Name/PIN

Credit Limit	Interest Rate	Customer Service	Notes

Section Five — Mortgage Information

First Mortgage

Company	Type	Interest Rate	Amount

Term Length	User Name/PIN	Website	Customer Service

Contact	Payment Address

Second Mortgage

Company	Type	Interest Rate	Amount
Term Length	User Name/PIN	Website	Customer Service
Contact	Payment Address		

Section Six — Rental Information

If you rent/lease your home, note your landlord's or rental company's information here.

Landlord	Rent	Date Due	End Date of Lease
Landlord Phone	Payment Address		

Section Seven — Student and Other Loans

Company	Type	Interest Rate	Amount
Term Length	User Name/PIN	Website	Customer Service
Company	Type	Interest Rate	Amount
Term Length	User Name/PIN	Website	Customer Service
Company	Type	Interest Rate	Amount
Term Length	User Name/PIN	Website	Customer Service

Section Eight — Insurance

Insurance Company	Member Number	Group/Policy Number	Customer Service
Type	Agent Name	Agent Number	Notes
Insurance Company	Member Number	Group/Policy Number	Customer Service

Type	Agent Name	Agent Number	Notes
Insurance Company	Member Number	Group/Policy Number	Customer Service
Type	Agent Name	Agent Number	Notes
Insurance Company	Member Number	Group/Policy Number	Customer Service
Type	Agent Name	Agent Number	Notes

Section Nine	Vital Documents

For this section, note the location of and any numbers or information for your vital documents. This includes birth, death, marriage certificates, green card, citizenship papers, passports, the deed to your house, wills, living trusts, any numbers or documents you might need to access in an emergency to prove your identification, citizenship or ownership of property.

Document	Numbers	Location
Contact/Agent	Phone	Notes
Document	Numbers	Location
Contact/Agent	Phone	Notes
Document	Numbers	Location
Contact/Agent	Phone	Notes
Document	Numbers (like citizenship/passport	Location
Contact/Agent	Phone	Notes

Section Ten	**Storage Unit/Safe Deposit Box**		
Bank or Storage Company	Address	Phone	Unit/Box #
Cost	Contents		Key Location
Bank or Storage Company	Address	Phone	Unit/Box #
Cost	Contents		Key Location

Section Eleven	**Income Payments (ie. Social Security or Retirement Benefits)**		
Source	Type of Benefit	Direct Deposit or Mail	Amount
Website	User Name/PIN	Contact	Customer Service #
Source	Type of Benefit	Direct Deposit or Mail	Amount
Website	User Name/PIN	Contact	Customer Service #

Section Twelve	**Memberships/ID Cards**		

In this section note any memberships you pay for, ie. the gym, professional organizations, book clubs, or other recurring payments

Gym Membership	Location	Member Number	Renewal Date
Other Membership	Location	Member Number	Renewal Date
Other Membership	Type	Member Number	Renewal Date

Section Thirteen	**Family Counselors**	
Attorney	Phone	Address
Email	Type	Call him/her for this type of information

Investment Counselor		Phone		Address		
Email		Type		Call him/her for this type of information		
Other Counselor		Phone		Address		
Email		Type		Call him/her for this type of information		
Other Counselor		Phone		Address		
Email		Type		Call him/her for this type of information		

Section Fourteen		**Important Passwords**			
Email Address #1	Log In URL	User Name	Password	Notes	
Email Address #2	Log In URL	User Name	Password	Notes	
Email Address #3	Log In URL	User Name	Password	Notes	
Social Site Account #1	Log In URL	User Name	Password	Notes	
Social Site Account #2	Log In URL	User Name	Password	Notes	
My Website #1	Log In URL	User Name	Password	Notes	
My Website #2	Log In URL	User Name	Password	Fee/Term	
File Storage Site	Log In URL	User Name	Password	Fee/Term	
Voice Mail #1	Dial In Number	Password	Instructions		
Voice Mail #2	Dial In Number	Password	Instructions		
Website	Log In URL	User Name	Password	What I use it for	

Family Evacuation & Location Plan

The Family Evacuation & Location Plan is the place for you to detail where you and your family will gather, and where you go if you have to evacuate your home or your area.

The Basics	Who Is Evacuating With You?

The Basics	Who Does What?

If a disaster or emergency occurred during the day while everyone was away from home, would anyone need help getting to the gathering location? Do you have children that need to be picked up or a loved one with special needs who will need physical help getting to the location? If so, detail those plans below, ie: Mary picks up kids, John picks up Grandpa.

Is there anything else that will need to be done by you or by a family member before or during the evacuation?

Section One	Local Gathering Place

If you and your family cannot gather at home after a disaster, but your immediate area is still safe, where will you meet?

Meeting Location (include address, phone and directions)

If this is a person's home, write in the name of person, phone number, and email address

Section One	Local Evacuation Location

If you and your family have to evacuate your home, but your immediate area is still safe, where will you live temporarily until you are allowed to go back home?

Local Evacuation Location (include address, phone and directions)

If this is a person's home, write in the name of person, phone number, and email address

Notes

Section Two	Out of Area Gathering Place

If you and your family cannot gather at home or in your immediate area/city after a disaster but your state is still safe, where will you meet?

Meeting Location (include address, phone and directions)

If this is a person's home, write in the name of person, phone number, and email address

Section Two	Out of Area Evacuation Location

If you and your family have to evacuate your home and your immediate area/city after a disaster, where will you live temporarily until you are allowed to go back home?

Out of Area Evacuation Location (include address, phone and directions)

If this is a person's home, write in the name of person, phone number, and email address

Notes

Section Three	Out of State Evacuation Location

If you and your family have to evacuate your home as well as your state/region, where will you go?

Out of State Evacuation Location (include address, phone and directions)

If this is a person's home, name of person, phone number, and email address

Alternate Location (include address, phone and directions)

If this is a person's home, name of person, phone number, and email address

Notes

Section Four	Transportation

How will we travel to evacuation location one?

How will we travel to evacuation location two?

How will we travel to evacuation location three?

Will you need to have any travel information with you, like maps, frequent flier or hotel membership numbers? If so note all of that information in the space below.

Section Five	Pets

Are there any pets evacuating with you? If yes, please list their names, breed and ages below

Vet # 1 Contact Information

Vet # 2 Contact Information

List the license information for your pets below, as well as the link to a current photo of your pet on your online file site or family web site. (photos are vital for identifying your pet if it were to become separated from the family)

If your pets are staying in a kennel during evacuation, note all of the information about the kennel below.

List any other information about your pet, ie. Immunizations, prescriptions, special instructions or medical information, below.			

Section Six		Our Family's Vital Life Lines	
Family's Web Site	Password	Online File Directory	Password
Facebook Site	My Space Site	Twitter Address	Other
Person	Email Address/IM Address	Person	Email Address/IM Address
Person	Email Address/IM Address	Person	Email Address/IM Address
Person	Email Address/IM Address	Person	Email Address/IM Address
Person	Email Address/IM Address	Person	Email Address/IM Address
Person	Phone Number	Person	Phone Number
Person	Phone Number	Person	Phone Number

GET YOUR
STUFF TOGETHER

Evacuation Checklist

On your Evacuation Checklist, list the items that you will be taking with you, the current location of the item and the name of the person responsible for gathering this item if you suddenly have to evacuate. In the first section, list anything you need to do before you leave the house, for instance turn off the gas or lock the door.

Section One — **Before I Leave The House I Need To…**

TASK	PERSON RESPONSIBLE

Section Two — **What Vital Items Do You Need To Take With You?**

ITEM	LOCATION	PERSON RESPONSIBLE
Family's Grab and Go Forms	Ready In 10 Notebook	Jane

Get Back To Life Plan

In this exercise you'll create a plan to help you take care of the following areas of your life in case you have to evacuate your home and are unable to live there for an extended period of time.

How will we handle our furniture or clothing needs?

How will we handle our bank accounts, paying our monthly bills and receiving our paychecks? How much emergency cash do we need to have, while traveling?

What are our credit card limits and toll free numbers for emergency increases?

How will we work? Will we work remotely or have to look for new positions? What people or contacts can we call about temporary or permanent jobs?

How will we handle our medical, dental and prescription needs while in the new location? What doctors and dentists can we use while there?

How long can we stay in our evacuation location? If we need to remain evacuated longer, where will we go/stay? Who will our real estate contacts be, if we need to find new permanent or temporary housing?

How are we going to secure the property or vehicles we had to leave behind?

How will we take care of our pets, during the evacuation and until we find new permanent housing?

How will we handle our transportation needs? What contacts will we need to purchase or lease vehicles?

How will we handle our daycare needs? How will we handle getting our children into school if necessary? What schools or contacts will we need, to enroll them in a new school in a temporary or new location?

How will we handle any special needs in our family?

This is how we will handle the following potential problems…

Write Out Your Plan As You Would Carry It Out

Write out your plan like this: During our evacuation we will stay in X location. I will be working remotely with my company laptop and our pets will be staying with Aunt Mary, just two blocks away. We will take care of our finances in this way…, so that you see a clear picture of where and how you will live while away from home.

Contacts You'll Need For Long Term Temporary Housing Or To Start Over

Name	Service	Phone/email	Notes

Financial Information

Section One	Bank Accounts		
Bank	Account Number	Branch	Checking/ Savings
Website	User Name/PIN	Customer Service	Notes
Bank	Account Number	Branch	Checking/ Savings
Website	User Name/PIN	Customer Service	Notes
Bank	Account Number	Branch	Checking/ Savings
Website	User Name/PIN	Customer Service	Notes
Bank	Account Number	Branch	Checking/ Savings
Website	User Name/PIN	Customer Service	Notes

Section Two	CDs and Investment Accounts		
Institution	Account Number	Branch	Investment Type
Broker/Counselor	Phone	Rate/Maturity Date	Notes
Institution	Account Number	Branch	Investment Type
Broker/Counselor	Phone	Rate/Maturity Date	Notes

Section Three		IRA/401K/Retirement Accounts		
Institution		Account Number	Branch	Type
Broker/Counselor		Phone	Notes	
Institution		Account Number	Branch	Type
Broker/Counselor		Phone	Notes	
Institution		Account Number	Branch	Type
Broker/Counselor		Phone	Notes	

Section Four		Credit Cards		
Company		Account Number	Website	User Name/PIN
Credit Limit	Interest Rate	Customer Service		Notes
Company		Account Number	Website	User Name/PIN
Credit Limit	Interest Rate	Customer Service		Notes
Company		Account Number	Website	User Name/PIN
Credit Limit	Interest Rate	Customer Service		Notes

Section Five	Mortgage Information		

First Mortgage

Company	Type	Interest Rate	Amount
Term Length	User Name/PIN	Website	Customer Service
Contact	Payment Address		

Second Mortgage

Company	Type	Interest Rate	Amount
Term Length	User Name/PIN	Website	Customer Service
Contact	Payment Address		

Section Six	Rental Information

If you rent/lease your home, note your landlord's or rental company's information here.

Landlord	Rent	Date Due	End Date of Lease
Landlord Phone	Payment Address		

Section Seven	Student and Other Loans

Company	Type	Interest Rate	Amount
Term Length	User Name/PIN	Website	Customer Service
Company	Type	Interest Rate	Amount
Term Length	User Name/PIN	Website	Customer Service
Company	Type	Interest Rate	Amount
Term Length	User Name/PIN	Website	Customer Service

Section Eight	Insurance

Insurance Company	Member Number	Group/Policy Number	Customer Service
Type	Agent Name	Agent Number	Notes
Insurance Company	Member Number	Group/Policy Number	Customer Service

Type	Agent Name	Agent Number	Notes
Insurance Company	Member Number	Group/Policy Number	Customer Service
Type	Agent Name	Agent Number	Notes
Insurance Company	Member Number	Group/Policy Number	Customer Service
Type	Agent Name	Agent Number	Notes

Section Nine — Vital Documents

For this section, note the location of and any numbers or information for your vital documents. This includes birth, death, marriage certificates, green card, citizenship papers, passports, the deed to your house, wills, living trusts, any numbers or documents you might need to access in an emergency to prove your identification, citizenship or ownership of property.

Document	Numbers	Location
Contact/Agent	Phone	Notes
Document	Numbers	Location
Contact/Agent	Phone	Notes
Document	Numbers	Location
Contact/Agent	Phone	Notes
Document	Numbers (like citizenship/passport	Location
Contact/Agent	Phone	Notes

Section Ten		Storage Unit/Safe Deposit Box		
Bank or Storage Company	Address	Phone	Unit/Box #
Cost	Contents		Key Location
Bank or Storage Company	Address	Phone	Unit/Box #
Cost	Contents		Key Location

Section Eleven		Income Payments (ie. Social Security or Retirement Benefits)		
Source	Type of Benefit	Direct Deposit or Mail	Amount
Website	User Name/PIN	Contact	Customer Service #
Source	Type of Benefit	Direct Deposit or Mail	Amount
Website	User Name/PIN	Contact	Customer Service #

Section Twelve		Memberships/ID Cards		

In this section note any memberships you pay for, ie. the gym, professional organizations, book clubs, or other recurring payments

Gym Membership	Location	Member Number	Renewal Date
Other Membership	Location	Member Number	Renewal Date
Other Membership	Type	Member Number	Renewal Date

Section Thirteen		Family Counselors	
Attorney	Phone	Address
Email	Type	Call him/her for this type of information

Investment Counselor		Phone		Address	
Email		Type		Call him/her for this type of information	
Other Counselor		Phone		Address	
Email		Type		Call him/her for this type of information	
Other Counselor		Phone		Address	
Email		Type		Call him/her for this type of information	

Section Fourteen		**Important Passwords**			
Email Address #1	Log In URL	User Name	Password	Notes	
Email Address #2	Log In URL	User Name	Password	Notes	
Email Address #3	Log In URL	User Name	Password	Notes	
Social Site Account #1	Log In URL	User Name	Password	Notes	
Social Site Account #2	Log In URL	User Name	Password	Notes	
My Website #1	Log In URL	User Name	Password	Notes	
My Website #2	Log In URL	User Name	Password	Fee/Term	
File Storage Site	Log In URL	User Name	Password	Fee/Term	
Voice Mail #1	Dial In Number	Password	Instructions		
Voice Mail #2	Dial In Number	Password	Instructions		
Website	Log In URL	User Name	Password	What I use it for	

GET YOUR
STUFF TOGETHER

Home Inventory

The Home Inventory was created to give you a place to record all of your valuable possessions, information about them, like model and serial numbers, warranty and the location of any additional information. In Step 10 of Ready In 10, you'll photograph those items or do a video tour of your home to show their original condition. If those items are ever lost or damaged, it would help you file an insurance claim. The Inventory is broken down by room and type of item.

Section One   Living Room

Item	Manufacturer	Model	Serial Number

Warranty Number	Expiration Number	Location of Photo/Link to Video Tour/Notes	

Item	Manufacturer	Model	Serial Number

Warranty Number	Expiration Number	Location of Photo/Link to Video Tour/Notes	

Item	Manufacturer	Model	Serial Number

Warranty Number	Expiration Number	Location of Photo/Link to Video Tour/Notes	

Item	Manufacturer	Model	Serial Number

Warranty Number	Expiration Number	Location of Photo/Link to Video Tour/Notes	

Item	Manufacturer	Model	Serial Number

Warranty Number	Expiration Number	Location of Photo/Link to Video Tour/Notes	

Item	Manufacturer	Model	Serial Number

Warranty Number	Expiration Number	Location of Photo/Link to Video Tour/Notes	

Item	Manufacturer	Model	Serial Number

Warranty Number	Expiration Number	Location of Photo/Link to Video Tour/Notes	

Item	Manufacturer	Model	Serial Number

Warranty Number	Expiration Number	Location of Photo/Link to Video Tour/Notes	

Section Two		Family Room/Den	
Item	Manufacturer	Model	Serial Number
Warranty Number	Expiration Number	Location of Photo/Link to Video Tour/Notes	
Item	Manufacturer	Model	Serial Number
Warranty Number	Expiration Number	Location of Photo/Link to Video Tour/Notes	
Item	Manufacturer	Model	Serial Number
Warranty Number	Expiration Number	Location of Photo/Link to Video Tour/Notes	
Item	Manufacturer	Model	Serial Number
Warranty Number	Expiration Number	Location of Photo/Link to Video Tour/Notes	
Item	Manufacturer	Model	Serial Number
Warranty Number	Expiration Number	Location of Photo/Link to Video Tour/Notes	
Item	Manufacturer	Model	Serial Number
Warranty Number	Expiration Number	Location of Photo/Link to Video Tour/Notes	
Item	Manufacturer	Model	Serial Number
Warranty Number	Expiration Number	Location of Photo/Link to Video Tour/Notes	
Item	Manufacturer	Model	Serial Number
Warranty Number	Expiration Number	Location of Photo/Link to Video Tour/Notes	
Section Three		Kitchen	
Item	Manufacturer	Model	Serial Number
Warranty Number	Expiration Number	Location of Photo/Link to Video Tour/Notes	
Item	Manufacturer	Model	Serial Number

Warranty Number	Expiration Number	Location of Photo/Link to Video Tour/Notes	
Item	Manufacturer	Model	Serial Number
Warranty Number	Expiration Number	Location of Photo/Link to Video Tour/Notes	
Item	Manufacturer	Model	Serial Number
Warranty Number	Expiration Number	Location of Photo/Link to Video Tour/Notes	
Item	Manufacturer	Model	Serial Number
Warranty Number	Expiration Number	Location of Photo/Link to Video Tour/Notes	
Item	Manufacturer	Model	Serial Number
Warranty Number	Expiration Number	Location of Photo/Link to Video Tour/Notes	
Section Four		**Master Suite**	
Item	Manufacturer	Model	Serial Number
Warranty Number	Expiration Number	Location of Photo/Link to Video Tour/Notes	
Item	Manufacturer	Model	Serial Number
Warranty Number	Expiration Number	Location of Photo/Link to Video Tour/Notes	
Item	Manufacturer	Model	Serial Number
Warranty Number	Expiration Number	Location of Photo/Link to Video Tour/Notes	
Item	Manufacturer	Model	Serial Number
Warranty Number	Expiration Number	Location of Photo/Link to Video Tour/Notes	
Item	Manufacturer	Model	Serial Number

Section Five	Office/Library		
Item	Manufacturer	Model	Serial Number
Warranty Number	Expiration Number	Location of Photo/Link to Video Tour/Notes	
Item	Manufacturer	Model	Serial Number
Warranty Number	Expiration Number	Location of Photo/Link to Video Tour/Notes	
Item	Manufacturer	Model	Serial Number
Warranty Number	Expiration Number	Location of Photo/Link to Video Tour/Notes	
Item	Manufacturer	Model	Serial Number
Warranty Number	Expiration Number	Location of Photo/Link to Video Tour/Notes	
Item	Manufacturer	Model	Serial Number
Warranty Number	Expiration Number	Location of Photo/Link to Video Tour/Notes	
Item	Manufacturer	Model	Serial Number
Warranty Number	Expiration Number	Location of Photo/Link to Video Tour/Notes	
Item	Manufacturer	Model	Serial Number
Warranty Number	Expiration Number	Location of Photo/Link to Video Tour/Notes	
Section Six	Dining Room/Additional Rooms		
Item	Manufacturer	Model	Serial Number
Warranty Number	Expiration Number	Location of Photo/Link to Video Tour/Notes	
Item	Manufacturer	Model	Serial Number

Warranty Number	Expiration Number	Location of Photo/Link to Video Tour/Notes	
Item	Manufacturer	Model	Serial Number
Warranty Number	Expiration Number	Location of Photo/Link to Video Tour/Notes	
Item	Manufacturer	Model	Serial Number
Warranty Number	Expiration Number	Location of Photo/Link to Video Tour/Notes	
Item	Manufacturer	Model	Serial Number
Warranty Number	Expiration Number	Location of Photo/Link to Video Tour/Notes	
Item	Manufacturer	Model	Serial Number
Warranty Number	Expiration Number	Location of Photo/Link to Video Tour/Notes	
Item	Manufacturer	Model	Serial Number
Warranty Number	Expiration Number	Location of Photo/Link to Video Tour/Notes	
Item	Manufacturer	Model	Serial Number
Warranty Number	Expiration Number	Location of Photo/Link to Video Tour/Notes	

Section Seven	**Property**		
Main Home	Insurer	Address	
Location of Ownership Documents		Location of Photo/Link to Video Tour/Notes	
Second Property	Insurer	Address	
Location of Ownership Documents		Location of Photo/Link to Video Tour/Notes	
Third Property	Insurer	Address	
Location of Ownership Documents		Location of Photo/Link to Video Tour/Notes	

Section Eight		Vehicles	
Type of Vehicle	Manufacturer	Model	EIN Number
Value/Purchase Date	Insurer	Mechanic Name/Number	
Location of Registration or Ownership Documents		Location of Photo/Link to Video Tour/Notes	
Type of Vehicle	Manufacturer	Model	EIN Number
Value/Purchase Date	Insurer	Mechanic Name/Number	
Location of Registration or Ownership Documents		Location of Photo/Link to Video Tour/Notes	
Type of Vehicle	Manufacturer	Model	EIN Number
Value/Purchase Date	Insurer	Mechanic Name/Number	
Location of Registration or Ownership Documents		Location of Photo/Link to Video Tour/Notes	
Type of Vehicle	Manufacturer	Model	EIN Number
Value/Purchase Date	Insurer	Mechanic Name/Number	
Location of Registration or Ownership Documents		Location of Photo/Link to Video Tour/Notes	

Section Nine		Jewelry
Item	Manufacturer	Value/Description
Insured By	Contact	Location of Photo/Link to Video Tour/Notes
Item	Manufacturer	Value/Description
Insured By	Contact	Location of Photo/Link to Video Tour/Notes
Item	Manufacturer	Value/Description
Insured By	Contact	Location of Photo/Link to Video Tour/Notes

Item	Manufacturer	Value/Description
Insured By	Contact	Location of Photo/Link to Video Tour/Notes
Item	Manufacturer	Value/Description
Insured By	Contact	Location of Photo/Link to Video Tour/Notes
Item	Manufacturer	Value/Description
Insured By	Contact	Location of Photo/Link to Video Tour/Notes
Section Ten	**Other Valuable Objects**	
Item	Manufacturer	Value/Description
Insured By	Contact	Location of Photo/Link to Video Tour/Notes
Item	Manufacturer	Value/Description
Insured By	Contact	Location of Photo/Link to Video Tour/Notes
Item	Manufacturer	Value/Description
Insured By	Contact	Location of Photo/Link to Video Tour/Notes
Item	Manufacturer	Value/Description
Insured By	Contact	Location of Photo/Link to Video Tour/Notes
Item	Manufacturer	Value/Description
Insured By	Contact	Location of Photo/Link to Video Tour/Notes

GET YOUR
STUFF TOGETHER

Quicklist

The Evacuation Quicklist contains any numbers that you might need in an emergency but who didn't make the cut on your vital information or medical forms. For example, the names of people you deal with every day, like good friends or your favorite service people. If you're evacuated, you might have to call your plumber or neighbor before you return, to look for damage to your home or take care of emergency repairs.

Additional Emergency Numbers

Name	Contact Type	Phone	Email	Notes
Name	Contact Type	Phone	Email	Notes
Name	Contact Type	Phone	Email	Notes
Name	Contact Type	Phone	Email	Notes
Name	Contact Type	Phone	Email	Notes
Name	Contact Type	Phone	Email	Notes
Name	Contact Type	Phone	Email	Notes
Name	Contact Type	Phone	Email	Notes
Name	Contact Type	Phone	Email	Notes
Name	Contact Type	Phone	Email	Notes
Name	Contact Type	Phone	Email	Notes
Name	Contact Type	Phone	Email	Notes

 **MEET THE WHOLE FAMILY**

You can find all of our books – both paperback and instant PDF downloads – on the Books tab of our website www.getyourstufftogether.com.

Get Our Books At Bulk Rates For Your Business, Church, Service Club or Organization! Email Us Through The Website For Details.

 **GET YOUR STUFF TOGETHER**

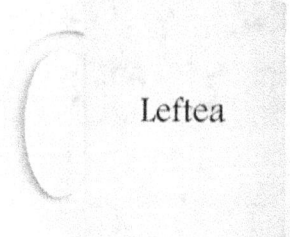

About The Authors

Janet and Laura are one of the only mother/daughter writing teams in the entertainment industry. They began their careers in production on network sitcoms at MGM and Warner Bros and are currently developing their own original movies and television series.

The Greenwalds were introduced to emergency preparedness the hard way, when a jumbo-jet crashed across the street from their home. But it was a horrendous medical tragedy – one that took the life of their mother/grandmother, Elaine Sullivan – that propelled them into new territory.

When Elaine's hospital failed to notify Jan and Laura of her hospitalization they were not only prevented from being at her side, but they were also kept from preventing the drug interaction that took Elaine's life.

After uncovering a loophole in the laws which regulate the notification of the next of kin of hospital patients, Laura & Jan joined forces with legislators in Illinois and California to enact three Next of Kin Laws, before creating Notify In 7, a training program that provides hospital professionals with the skills they need to notify and reunite trauma victims with their loved ones, quickly and easily. Hoping to keep other families from experiencing the same thing they had, they turned their story into a screenplay called Without Consent, now in development as a feature film.

Their book *Keep Everything You Love Safe*, gives readers quick and easy steps they can take to keep everything that's important to them organized, safe and accessible. Each section – over 30 in all – covers a different area from backing up & fixing family photos, home movies and music, to creating an evacuation plan, securing vital documents, medical information, financial information and data.

Between their books, blog and website, over 1.5 million people have used Jan and Laura's shortcut sheets, action plans and materials to keep themselves, their homes, their families and the things that they love, safe and secure.

www.ingramcontent.com/pod-product-compliance
Lightning Source LLC
Chambersburg PA
CBHW081412280526
45788CB00009B/3066